OUT OF NOWHERE

OUT OF NOWHERE

poems by

Susan Comninos

STEPHEN F. AUSTIN STATE UNIVERSITY PRESS

ISBN: 978-1-62288-237-3

Production Manager: Kimberly Verhines
Book design by Sandra Carranza
Cover photo by Jack Gittoes, Pexels
Author photo by Lana Ortiz

For more information:
Stephen F. Austin State University Press
P.O. Box 13007 SFA Station
Nacogdoches, TX 75962
sfapress@sfasu.edu
www.sfasu.edu/sfapress
936-468-1078

Distributed by Texas A&M University Press Consortium
www.tamupress.com

For my family

Rabbi Simeon says: "It is all so mysterious, these events and emotions that appear out of nowhere, that are given to us, perhaps without our consent."

— Stephen Mitchell, "Lamentations"

[Still] even in August, in early darkness, I am responsible / for these vines.

— Louise Glück, "Vespers"

CONTENTS

OUT OF NOWHERE

BEQUEATHAL

If legacy means long arms —
my grandfather's smile
stitched to the gap

in my teeth, then
when I die, make
me a golem

from a palmful
of dirt and torn
pocket of time, with arms

long enough to reach
you, to play
with the fringes at your waist.

OUR FATHER, OUR KING

I don't feel like a cherished girl. The fall
enters as a forgiven guest, known to the dinner party, if absent
for seasons. Our father, our king, the air is full of tolerant embraces.
Trees thrust out their branches, and I cannot
do my part. Our father, why
have you brought me into your orchard of plums? To show me
the autumnal variety? I am well-versed
in the sight of fruit
as it stacks in pails. What good does it do
you, to show me faultless things? You are fast losing
my most faithful sense
of your indifference. Our king, for years, I have known you
as you claimed to be: wrathful, or dispassionate, but always at a good
distance. Now you torment me with nearness. Take
your hand from my head; I'll uncover
my eyes, I'll testify
to your off-kilter beauty. Without direction, I'd recall for a jury:
this harvest is more lovely and worthy
of exhibit than the most mature
and idiosyncratic among your works. I swear,
I curse. I ask for a remission
of words, and to be left in an unenlightened
silence. Or, as you once did
with ribs, reconsider
my exquisite oneness, which
you created. May you see fit
to deliver me an unwashed
and distinctly wicked man. May you make him offensive

as an apple eater, a clothes wearer, a sky-fisting
bellower, but send me a dirty beloved,
whose body will drop down, distend
and discharge like an overripe berry
into my knowledged mouth.

RUSTIC IMPRESSION
of a blind house, a barn, and forked path

At first, the flowers open
to a scene that makes us stay
fixed on its slate roofs, the drop

from their eaves to the two
skewed red doors, one hung
on a bespectacled barn. Its

windows stare right
at a whitened house: the lone
blemish, a blood slab of wood.

No barrow depends on this
trio of hens — or are they
cocks? — strutting, wattles

rouged as poppies
blurred to a haze near
a cadre of rocks. Like

blunt cadets, they point
to a crotch in the yard. It spreads
its branched bones in the dirt

then cracks out a path
between hay and home, table
and trough. Unlovely

letter, it wants us to name
what we are: cad or cluck. At our best
loved, we scratch down

a dirt road to sleep, beasts
bound for their separate
beds. Plucked from paint to be

a bird or a man, we perch on
respective clawed feet: all to march
for one hanged pair of doors.

NAKED ADMISSION: A FANTASY

that the nudists who took a predawn tour of Palais
de Tokyo instead chose to visit the Louvre

I imagine the nudists rising
early to eat cheese, drink
café au lait before
heading — all points
checked with their enfleshed *fraternité*,
their closest art-loving *copains* —
for the Louvre. To stare at torsos
and busts, laid in no-touch halls
with conditioned air, they must first
stop meeting *au sous-sol* —
where walls sport bleu veins
found on Roquefort flights, each
wedge as bottom-heavy as
an Anjou pear. So, launched like rafts,
hosts of naturists ride, all limbs and
padded seats on the Metro, zipped
in their maps of skin. Some hang
from questionably cleaned
poles. Others walk down the moist
morning streets, with unprotected backs
and hair. It's a show: of bodies
hydraulically graced
by youth — and of others, freed
from the clothes that function
like slings. Sagging no more
at their exclusion from sights
like the Mona Lisa in pain — suffering
her societal ache: tooth

gripped by a tongue that will soon
be unstrapped, to lick a cut
on the thumb, or juice from the lips
after eating — our naked fellows,
our coterie of curated
corps, designed by DNA, spread
among the art. Then in homage
to a wired tour guide, they clot
in a klatch of courteous ears
worn above stirred, then
shrunken chests. Like iron lungs
puffed with air, the nudists become
so pure — like marbled installations, rarely
moved: near-statues, poised
in a Gallic light — unbleached
by windows set too high
to mar   their original
breathing portrait
of skin.

DURING COVID, SHE DREAMS OF LEAVING
A MASKED MAN

and then after, telling him why

Because we were the bones
of bees   and too fragile

to last beyond the hive:
that basket of simple   buzzing

Because everything about salt
and jab was precisely   what I liked

Because your skin and mine
had become   a contamination

Because I could stroke the air
more readily than I could   your throat

Because I wanted to sing
you to sleep   with my fingers

Because the nights droned on
like fire alarms: terrible   but necessary

Because you were an everyday
apple, become   a near-consumed fruit.

ASCENT

Places that will not want
You, strike hooves below the earth.
Fur-breathed, and winter friendly—

Cider and hot baths,
Like consolation, cool
Off fast. Why, Kafka,

Have I had so little
In common with myself?
Only the moon could know

How sly I feel, gaping
At its glut of stars.

ARCTIC TRAVELER
for the fox that walked 2,700 miles across melting ice

Little fox, how long will you stay
in my imagination, steadily
traipsing toward dawn? Put

down your silvered coat
and jaw, mined from your den
in Norway. Lick your nailed paws. For

millennia, you've been stored,
my needle-nosed plier, among
hammers of your Arctic

home: antlered reindeer,
clawed bears and weaponized
salmon, flung hard

as peppered snow, made errant
by dirt. But when ice warms,
it reconstitutes

in darts — as sharp
as you, brave tooth. So
what did you prise

from home's belly
when you left it for colder
cold: its myths of fish? What

taste kept you slipping
across continents, meted
in miles, from your glossed

caps in sunlight, all
summer — to this
Canadian post? Soldier

dodging an end to your
epoch among Swedes,
Danes, and Finns (and their *bêtes*

noires: the Russians), unhook
your red tongue. Then wash
till night turns you

into a sickle, an almost
closed o. Sleep in my stunned
mind, softer than your body —
bent on glaciered roads.

A LOVE POEM
for my mother

Adonai of night and of flowers,
God of my life. I was not expected to be
beautiful. When flowers grew from my hands, I surprised everyone
but my mother.

In any language my name
means *lily*. Basin in a vase
or bath of rain, I have the same wholly American
whorls (fingerprints, curls), and features as when
my first-generation mother
invited me into being
her future. She asked, and I answered
with a face like her mama's
mishpokhe, but with different colored
petals: my hair, oh my eyes.

A NEW YORK SKETCH
for David

The undone shoes in your pied-à-terre
Face down my luggage on stumped feet:

Dachshunds of Samsonite, mute and laid bare
Beneath hangers. We leave only to eat.

No glance from your model
Night doorman: no wink, frère to frère,

In heat. The lobby is empty
Of dog owners, mail and the other

Tight-roped walkers — toothsome fakers
Like ourselves. *What are we? Darling?* Wear

The beard on your lips like brocade
On a hispid chair. My hand strokes the mate

To a door's lock, gone into at length: far
From the promise of your paper jamb and frame.

CHIROPTERA
after she's been left at the altar

My dazed face stares like a bat
hidden in a cave of hair.
A rat's nest smells of rat.
My lonely squeak of "I'm stuck here;
come back," holds me upside down
in my jizz-sprayed gown.

Inside, I'm foul-mouthed. I sway
left to right, my love
of lockjaw displayed.
Hygiene's a lace glove
I dropped like a Spanish pronoun.
In my jizz-sprayed gown

I hang, foot then foot: fanged husk
on a spit of webbed thread.
Now, we're embroidered, musk
to muzzle. Now we're bed
to bean, face to stone eiderdown.
In my jizz-sprayed gown

I'm drenched with seltzer:
mineral fizz. I'm strung
out on dripping, "melts her
when she spots it" rock. Wrung
from stalactites, droplets drown.
In my jizz-sprayed gown

I wrap up the walls
of my velvet wings. The sleaze
from my flapping stalls —
stops on a hostel breeze.
My stays are half-star renowned
in my jizz-sprayed gown.

I take ruined rooms as loans.
From belfry to glue
on the underside of a roan's
swelled gut, I'm a stuck shoe.
No worn horn rips me down
in my jizz-sprayed gown.

PECAN, RODEF, CLAM

like any nut zipped up
tight in its shell. like a clam's
clipped *momser*, the locked
maw talked open
by fire: by burly water
waitressing flesh, flat as a tongue,
to sterile plates. under fissures, a
soft sloth, holy fruit, hare
-lipped by cleavers:
the devil's hand. sweet
meat of the tree. bone
boy, edible kernel, marrow
of roots, hung up
on earth. like a palmed
pit, disappeared
into its own
stone jacket. loony
seed in brittle furniture: lone
in a rooming house; even
halved, only
one twin per womb.

AUGUST BLUES
in July

Five a.m. and I've been
Up since four
With the clamoring
Birds, and an owl whose
Five-beat hoot disputes
My claim of the day
Before that the Blues
Puts faith in four
Beats — eloquent
As a bar can get.

BEAR SPOTTED IN DELMAR
headline from a small-town newspaper

I imagine your breath smells —
though I've never seen you close

enough to sniff you, or even
wave to you from a window

of a car, piloted by me or another
daylight driver. Though once, long

ago, at summer camp, I saw a horse
wipe its dripping snot on a girl's

sheer skirt. It was more of a slide
than a swipe, but still. We shrieked.

The girl never returned: she'd been
dismissed for her behavior —

a tale that went unshared
with the bulk of us, left snorting

at the hinted story. So why
does your foray into town

seem funnier than any news
I've read today? You've emerged before

in various guises — suitor with an accent;
a lost clown in Groucho Marx glasses —

all through the state
of banked hay and confusion

that can mark a rural life. Pity the ripe
bear, grabbing at loaves

of stone-soft bread from the counter
of growled hopes: at the scent

of stale humor, thin mockery
and rank, timid despair. It will go hungry.

WORDS FROM A MIDWEST FARM WIFE
for a traveling circus acrobat

You swing here from the East
where nothing is dusty —

just diesel and domes. Where
church spires are syringes

flushed from earth like
strung-out doves, pinpricked

vessels of stupor. Here, cows
cluster in gangs. They chaw

and low. I wish you'd unhook
my blouse, sewn from spit

and calico. But aloft, you sweat
your way through your spiraling

grabs: hand, twist, air — hand.
The dumb meat weight of you

pikes, curls back on itself
like a peeled plum's skin —

one scared to be caught
staring by the knife. Still

what's left to risk, or fear? Fists,
maybe. Rope burn. The perpetual

stink of pigs and tractor grease. More
bars like the one you hang from,

showman. But the Big Top's got
spicier acts than you. Lions seethe

on their stools, their tails like scythes
to slash wheat. And clowns boil

from their red-hot car. They pop
and roll like bath plugs, yanked

from scalded sinks. So, what
would it take for you to blister

your own way down
past the net — the shock

on our Midwestern faces? Are you brave
enough to strike

up a homestead here, in the flattest
form of sky? Fall upwards

at us, like haystacks made you
some sawdust promise: that a girl

would catch you in her
burlap sack. No greater show

on earth: not milk barns. Not flies.
No need to scream on your arrival.

IMAGINING ABRAHAM
as my silent immigrant parent

My father was a wandering Aramean;
he placed a dead deer in my hands.

My father was a wandering Aramean
and erased for me the path to his home.

My father was a wandering Aramean
whose goodness was the oar that rowed him

in the boat of his soul. Alone

my father was an Aramean. He
spotted the dark in blurred halos,

my father. Was an Aramean wandering
because he'd been cast out by beasts?

My father wandered. Like an Aramean —
his feet were his indigent's shoes.

He unveiled himself
to the air like a shivering bride.

My father, my wanderer,

walked on the ice near our home
like a heron. My father

was ice of the lake, a bird
of sparse plumage. He wandered, as feathers

fly.

AT THE DOG PARK, LATE

At this place, where the dogs bark and run,
and the sun is largely gone, and the day
has cooled, two trucks slowly circle this
park within a park, alone in a spit

of grass, and the weeds that stop up
holes. At their lowest point, along a chain
-link fence, the green climbers know that
all windows must be grown through

or blocked. It is late, and the air is soft:
quiet, but for the sound of two motors
and of gravel scraped: that roughed-up
grind, when a car doesn't stop. My dog

races for the road, pantomimes a social
call: his card laid on an imaginary plate,
set beside a public water bowl. First, one
man creeps his rig; then the next. They trawl

for drugs or sex — or ticks to take
home to their wives. What more
could they possibly want? A kill
in the ocean? To eat kelp, as open

-mouthed as whales, unabashed by their
shared appetite? Drivers, there's
nothing here, but a woman
and her dog: both small and dumb

enough to sit and wait —
for the bones of explanation to be tossed,
like a ringing phone, at their feet — or to gnaw
at their own, honed stubbornness. Say, "Go!"

and the pair will stay, only later to speak
of what there was to be gained — knowledge,
witness, pain? — an ending for the story. A
ghosting of intention, before it was gone.

PALEONTOLOGY

Something about a fossil that churns up
tenderness. Its soft essence filleted
and inhumed frame exposed. The rules of first
note are: you aim for a ruin. Though the stone
ferns of absent spines *don't have to* crumble.
If you go at them blunt-fingered, you'll get
streaked with hieroglyphics. Sediment will
scrape and tarnish your hands. To reveal that
prior health, you have to rub against rock.
The quarrel's between earth and enduring
will. Well-preserved life doesn't talk back as
chaos. And calcified diamonds grant
value, as the vanished. You love the rare
notion of the generous skeleton:
the physics it lent to an ambulant
mass. Now dead weight's been loosed and the floorplan
fled. Casual as epochs, dungareed
with dirt, you dig and raise catacombs
of huge, passé birds; perhaps rigid beasts
with hair; or miniature-limbed swimmers who
essayed an entrée onto anhydrous
land. Let the thumbprints of bodies remain
free of blood. Let the science you unearth
be of the desiccant and the cold. And
then it becomes just a matter of bone.

RIGOR CELSIUS
in Central New York

I'm allotted winter, allowed
Nothing that wasn't before. Still, I am

Hovering a hand, tender to banks
    of precipitate. May
Our next day be beset by
Nocturnal mountains and stinging stars. Like this
Opinion, snowdrifts? This danger-of-us eclipsing
Rheumy streets and practical plows? Let's

Aid only the air: Mock heat
    of liquid
Nitrogen. A helium head flares up
Down in a New York valley. Lift

Praise, shovels and skiers,
Rueful noses and itchy-pant aches. After
All (this temperate, tolerable year), the ice
Is so insistent —
    insensate, specific; flaying tongues that slip
Smart answers to cells
    of the metal
Element: its shrill decree
    that decades and octaves
        drop forever
            gallons below.

DECONSTRUCTION WORKERS

I find you under the holly, become
a Christian sprig, I admit,
but then there is
a conversion of berries
into a kind lightning rod

that transfers electric
jolts to our genus. Linguists
of the shrub variety
make waxy a mate
to verdant. Green's the grace

most of us would like. To miss
you netted by needles
is to have the foresight
of a wood pest, eating
what builders won't abate —

blind. Termites
have the idea; they take
what's hard to a
softer state. All
those amendments

that might be made: soaking
our structures with spit
till the holly's left
hanging, anfractuous —
beams busting the house out of halves.

ITALIAN FOR YOU
cooking for Antonio

Some give up their skins
easily, but you slipped

a gourd, glanced sideways
at the past, welled up like a gorge

with flirty water. I was young
as miracles, when I was afloat

before *frustrated*. Sound
gabbles up like flames, like ice

shrills off a liminal map. My flight
across the Swiss peaks, so close

to the sun, the blond Alps —
like gold teeth — guarded gates

to Malpensa (o night of Europe, o red
eye, and stiff neck). Strange thought, I left

what's known to melt into
stew: bare beef, and armpit

of scent; this lure of the grist,
of the grind; this evening spent; this

myth ended without mint — in stir
and in season (tomato,

fat and meat) — in
you: oh, delicious descent.

LULLABY
for a husband

Taking the Eros
out of it, I admire
your wool shirt, your wallet

which is worn and lithe.
Green like any tea life
likes to be. Black

with its color. Beneath
you, I think of afghans,
a winter of blankets: cold

compress that the
heat's left. This room
has cracked

around the windows, or through
the walls —
if there were ever.

Your hand is like
the craters of the earth.
I fall into it.

COMMITMENT

Call it rocky
land, a slim raft
of hope, a shimmied
then stagnant skiff, squatting
in the shallows, visibly

rapt, longing at the shore.
Its anchor has the taste
of iron, when you gnaw
at the leg of its length,
then haul it up, link over

married link: capable, strong.
Feel it, this boat
of boredom turns fast
as a fish, gulping
happiness as gladly

as it does the patinaed air. Puffed,
its gills push us far
from its ears
like a fight, too wet
and fixed to recall. A hook

to the mouth pulls us
close, almost
to the center
of something. You dive
your drift onto it, then me.

INTAGLIO
winter, in front of the TV

Oh, gray-hair:
Arm of speckled boredom,
Sit awhile
And pull your throat
A cask of some
-thing Peculiar.

The villagers are coming.
Let's smile
With straws
And other
Cupboard staples.

Thief. Shoeless wonder.
The drop-cloth
Of the window strains
The yellow
Light.

Oh, poked moon.
You like a flayed field,
Hinged-hipped in the house
Strays built for stones
To live in.

BEES, YOU, AND A BIRD DREAM
a poem in collage

"Overturned Truck Spills Millions of Bees on the Highway"
—*TIME magazine headline on hives bound for a farm in Washington State*

Bees

They were brought in by truck
To taste the salt air. Witless
Sommeliers, gunned by instinct, sip
By stricken sip, they were bombed

Up the West coast. Ocean,
  what's

Your riven call
To ride? A cult-like moan:
Settle utopia, known
For garage-bands: so

Loud.

I don't like the sound, but I love the air
Crying in from the window.

You

Once, in sleep, your ear was a sunken bowl,
Filled with stones I'd never see.
Every breath: not a drum — but silent;
Brassy; unstrung —

A solo of small instruments.

When littleness matters, each
Sting makes some cracked,
Pebbled sense.

Bird

This morning, a cardinal
— his dark eyes matched by his harlequin mask —
Dropped like a beaked
Anvil, at my feet.

Dream

And those bees, benighted
Pilgrims, emptied
As overturned bags,
In the street. Their crawl:

Like mosaic —

A glass face, beaten
To a savage whole. Then pricked

Like a fissured pane, still shut. Last night:
Your absence on the water was a swept, black wing. Then

I was a bird, wanted
Away, and pecking out.

CHILDLESSNESS
per il mio ex amore

I guess it's an affectation:
The boat you slip into
When you flee the night. The sea's
Awake with insulin. What does it mean
That I dream of you, still
Crossing palms, lawns, the laws
Of language suspended? Drop your accent
On a female line of wash.
Pin me in place. Your
Wine from old grapes
And men in shirtsleeves
Keeps me sick on morsels
From another life: parchment, wafers
Like paper, loss. How
I loved you, in your derelict
Boots, your sweat
-stained limbs, your
Rancid misuse of a
Horse. As my time
For a child fled, you
— *il mio dolce codardo* —
Thought bride and bridle
Fit the same.

A COED'S BIRTHDAY
marked by her college clock tower

Nothing happened. But the rain
jerked from the sky, then jaywalked
toward earth, while dim light
stroked the eyelids of excited
clouds, clamped with an ardor
against the day. Even now, a stomach
draws a knot — recalls the daft
butterflies, the dense wind
that blew a backdrop
of gravitas for girly
wings (for *frappés* beat
by crazed foundlings: the moths
in the updraft). It's serious
foul weather, when the dew lifts
its anvil upwards to strike
whatever's walking. Upright
dongs a bell, whose deaf tones
ruin the chorus of rain. Rip back
a corner on this failed sheet
which, note by note, wants
to mate with the trees, the damned
grass, the shiftless roofs. Nothing
sweet starts like this — lover
of branches, by posting
amorous intentions
on the short-waved air —
but moss, and the mud. You'll die

in the hooves and hair
of animals that move slow
and eat up the expanse
of the soiled ground. But, for you, wet
friend, nothing happened.

I DON'T THINK HE HAD ANY INTENTION TO HIRE
after Philip Levine

since the clock ticked so discretely
That daylight ebbed down

Without the squeak of drawers, or remote
Clack of computer keys. No

Sound of work — no workers — passed
Through his doors, like a bomb

Packed in a bag, waiting for time
To go off. Explosively, he exhaled,

Drummed shut a thought, held
Wound a fact, favored a

Posture of parsimony. "This
Business is coming back," he

Said, before shaking and
Swiveling me out. "We'll

Be in touch." He lightly scaled
The sounds, touched the back

Of my hope, scurried: a shame
-faced guest, its pilled coat

Unbuttoned. His words hung like
Dust motes, tossed from his lungs

Into boredom, their flat music straining
My shoulders, marring the prosperous air.

CREED: A STILL LIFE

Acceptance is the graph paper of youth.
Chart disappointments on it. That's what I do.

The fruit fly's a minor chord lifting above
the stove on its drunken flight to

Nothing. Nowhere. Its looped rise, a theme
the whole kitchen sways against, says, "Do

what you like to switch the fall lights on." The leaves,
like traffic bulbs, flash their creed: green, go

red. Who's confused? No one wants the fruit
of the vine, once the table grapes dry. Do

you think that they'll keep? They never do.
Here's a tune for this tableau: love

the worm, the wine, the swell of the lip
of the vase in a darkening room. Stay

sweet, overripe. Put cloth on your head
like you're the blessed bread. Pour milk by feel. Stop

the blind exit of husband, sons,
the boys who drove to see you. Do

grope your way past this wreck of a door,
this apple-wracked scene. Can

you know me now, waving at you? Break this frame: last,
first, and through the stricken middle. Leave it. Do.

APPLES

When there's fruit
There will be flies. The
Truth comes as I wash
My hands above a sink,
Infested with activity.

RAW SPRING
on noticing a maple branch in March

Buds fist their way
Open: polyamorous

Display

Of thumbs, pushing
Pulp, in cold light. Say

Each threesome spawns
Six sores, poked at heaven —

Rakes

Low birds, thrusts
Red nubs:

     shaved

Tonsils, spat in flight.
Crouch and sway,

Chafe

And shove, muted
Buttons. Grind away.

Then speak rude
To power: *Hey!*

You arrogant
Flowers

Splay leaves
Like fingers; shaft

This day.

SONNET FOR A WART ON MY HAND

Thickened nail, thumb
of fat instinct: flip
on the bum-bum
ick in my chest. Blip
of angst, strip
off. Ruined digit, gummed
gutter of skin: lip
to finger. Mum
on skewed cells, numb
crust over flesh. Rip,
shed as you might, your hummed
scales are worn, parasite. Crumb
of gesture, flick off your face
to hide, under nail, where you warp and waste.

QUESTION FOR THE SAGES
a plague poem in spring

In this time of hallelujah
to little and nothing — except
for the bluebells that keep rising
from the moist dirt by a dumpster
emptying its belly of gifts to the gods
of recycling and carbon emissions,
and wafting scent to the jaunty paws
of the dogs within us, who know that
rank and the warm body are *now*, and little
can our snoots forget what they were
meant to praise, and really — my
God (my earthly, succulent
one) — all faith in flowers, and in
mud: why should they?

BACK DOOR
or, sonnet of cheating with a friend's man

Something about the hinge
of your hips, the way you held them straight

when you danced. You pushed my palm to fringe:
the pelt of your belly, then sought the gate

you'd take into my body. Slick
as a wet floor that ruins

suede shoes — the sand tick
that hangs on from sea dunes

and back — you imagined a door
tucked between two wounds, then pushed

there. "Choose," I said, before
you slid backwards to try ruched

skin. "Not that," I said, meaning that I knew
that I loved nothing — neither her, nor you.

WE HAVE TRESPASSED
song of the slim girls, starved

We have trespassed; we have dealt treacherously
with our desire, coercing a rebirth from bone;

we have acted perversely; we have done wrong
in our bodies, wishing them hollow as folly;

we have robbed; we have spoken slander
against the grown, women full of the mind;

we have been presumptuous; we have done violence
to ourselves, to our own candied forms;

we have practiced deceit; we have counseled evil
before mirrors, exhorting by example;

we have revolted; we have blasphemed
our wombs to slivers, no blood tricked from ivory;

we have spoken falsehood; we have scoffed
at the edible, animal that it is;

we have rebelled; we have committed iniquity
only in a doze, that nodding boy, who alone knows our skin;

we have been stiff-necked, we have acted wickedly
as sexless pixies, before their hair grows in;

we have transgressed; we have oppressed
appetite, our sentient caterwaul;

we have dealt corruptly; we have committed abomination
as old as the science that declared the earth round;

we have gone astray; we have led others astray —
off the world's abdomen, as we found it, flat.

UNPLOTTED

after William Wordsworth's "Nuns Fret Not"

Within the sonnet's scanty plot of ground
someone sings off-tune. Someone's plotted
novel flips off-road. Someone's plot to leave
a neutral town — paved over, by shift in plot
to a storied house, with trees. The plotted room
— mute office in the wake of the plotted degree —
unrented, undrawn, reverse-plotted. For sake of
vinting, local-sourcing, ecopoverty — whatever the plot —
instead plot what happens: backyards; gardens; cook
-outs, camp; children's freshly pillowed heads. Plot
even the snipped poms of plotted stalks: roses
rushing towards the dawn of the domestic plot —
the rise of the plotted drowned, briefly shining
in prosody's time, before the freshly dug plot.

MARCH
or, deteriorating vision at 50

Misery follows you like a foot
too big for its shoe: a miscalculation
wiggling its toes, without intent

to go bald in the granular snow.
Your eyes start to read language
wrong: *cheese* becomes *Chinese*; the gaffe

scurrying — on blind circuitry. Even
steel wool develops a scrape
like grief, like cast iron struck

against the pan of oiled thought. Why
wax dramatic, when a line break's just
a raveled hem on the leg: that kicks

past the front door, the ice-nailed
stoop, and the battered, winter trees? What's
stitched to this felt framework is form. What's
left to the dark? — the sundowned week.

MAX HEADROOM, IN MIDLIFE, DROPS
DOUBTFUL ADVICE ON HIS SON

Maybe there'll be nothing left —
maybe there won't be. A tic feels

more real than the body,
the head looks more whole

than the whole. Blank sheets
of rain slick a torso of snow,

wet stitches the ground above
ground. It's grand, how music

splayed in arcs, from cave to mp3
to I don't know. I stopped caring

with college. Time rolls: in waves (soldiers
of fortune, but distracted — furious

with boredom). Attention's a lapse,
it lacks focus. See

how slowly the sun dials back
its hot face, at our frowns? Don't

stop dissing puffs of clouds:
Who are they to talk-talk

like ghosts of gassed-up whimsy?
The air is dosing. Wake it

with a needled presence, your
nattering voice. Unhook an earpiece,

throw me the tatters of your banter.
H-h-here is the hear that you've longed for.

AUDITORY TUNE

I've been digging too much in my ears,
Sweet dears. Apricots make me turn
For the closed cupboard door. They lick
Me like a spoon. They tell of iron, of A,
Of scanning the dark for the Chesapeake
Floor. Flesh, twist me to one knee–
hold on your banks of dried and stored.
Grab onto this grin of shame: you
Shed skin on my jaw. Chew, or smile? Starved
Popularity's a priest on the moor. Sing cowls
And of coils, my solitary bowl. Forgive me my
Sticky half-heart. Turn your heard back on me.

WANTED:

An arranged marriage,
The dowry a hot bundle

Of cloth. Gold
As lemon dawn, the sky

Unfurled: a cooked up
Bolt of silk. Up close,

Its threads should be vapor —
But from a distance,

A lens: forged to set
Ants on fire. All insects

Start to dance
On igniting; each

Loss sparks
Off another. Look:

There goes a body
Now, its painted

Jeans smoking, aglow —
One halo backlit

By stars, ready
To run the block down.

EVENING IN DAYLIGHT

Consider it hung,
Consider it hanged.

The day concluding immensely
Across the sky, strafed by white

Bandages. A blanket
Abstraction — diphthong

At its center — one lettered stage
Right; stage left. Stars'll be made

To rise up later: post-nude
Shines on a baby blank

Page. Their lit lungs
Alight, each blued-up

Flame's a rise: each gassed
-out flame's descendant.

UPSTATE, APRIL

This spring loves me like blood, crazy
for my wrists and hands. It pulses
thin in its green misgivings. I admit
I'm surprised by its strict evocation
of water: mud, red bruises of swollen tissue —
xylem, phloem — the usual affair. But I'm ready
for winter to lift its beard off the
scraping ground. The whole sky
has done its penance. Listen: even the eighteen wheelers
seem grateful in their grinned gunnings past.
The highway distant, all loads are
a good-graced thrumming. Sound's
the survivor here. Through winter
it's been shutting us up with an absence, groaning
within the hardpan ground,
giving us all a bad rap for our bones,
hurting us with a hardness
of hearing: this soliloquy of loss.
We're better, now,
with our dingy faces clearing like a high-ground mark on the hills —
I can see them, as they've always been: painful, there,
awkward as drunkards fumbling —
denuded, then wreathing, green-full:
thrusting wet, sharped needles, all fir
writhing upwards towards the brim.

WIDOWS AND ORPHANS
for weeds gone blowzy

Dandelions don't have petals
Plucked to feel, or not
For your palm. Just

As a spit of chance, they
Navigate the air,
Shirred, sired —

Held, held, held,
Then bossed: done. Sent
To the tindered

Lawn, the burnt, brown
Loam. Dirt: do it. Now
See what's been puffed. Play gone.

IS IT

a drunk writer wonders on her 50th birthday

necessary to be strange
to be a poet? Well, it helps. I hear
it helps. But what about this
ghost you greet
once a year: bombed
mosquito at your
back, always cha-cha-ing
with ice to irk you. What about
her? Isn't she
strange? Yes, but in her lush
way, she whines a glass
on your table. Normalcy's
in that. Strange is something
else: like shut drapes, the cut
canvas moon, slunk to the floor
of a boarded house. You're a monster
there. Your fear is what
turns the cranks. Every window
is the one you push
past, for the scarlet air. You're dead.
You're a body with a head. A
rag dipped in bony words. Now
go and write.

BEACHED, OR DEMENTIA

nothing tender, nothing
taught beside my skin. naught
for hindrance, all for ale —

for fizzy friskness. for persimmon
taste, for *tsimmes*. woe
to the freak snail, the squid

in its sea-boiled soul. for this
i grow and swim? by mist i
shift my husk to sand. adrift

in absence, the brain, swell
upon swell, falls a slip. the pail's
knocked over, the spade's gone

from its hilt. the waves slop
out: spent, ridiculous. they
set themselves assailed.

SUDDENLY

Last night, I dreamed of a dead poet and a widower who suddenly became available. I don't mean that being bound up in love preoccupies us — to the point where we cease to be a body unattached by a cord of cells to the shape of another person's soul (though perhaps that's really true) — but instead, an emotional face that's been wiped clean of tribute, freed from pretending we don't sometimes wish: that our lot lived on a parallel tract; that half of our lives were buried elsewhere, in a different plot of the cemetery; that suddenly, we believed in resurrection, if that means getting to loiter on a dented street corner, cigarette dangling from our shopworn lips: we, the young stranger, who happens, suddenly, to be us. What I mean is: in this dream I had been hungry a long time, admired for eons, yet starved, and, suddenly, the two funerals meant that I could eat. There was enough oxygen in the room for just one battered body, and, suddenly, I was it. No one else stopped breathing, but it was clear that the table — however tempting it wasn't, with its stale victuals: that stunningly silly word — suddenly had just one seat available, and that it would, just as suddenly, go to me.

GLOSSARY

au sous-sol — in the basement (French)

bêtes noires — objects of aversion; enemies (French)

café au lait — coffee with milk (French)

Chiroptera — mammalian order of bats; winged hands (Latin)

copains — friends (French)

frappés — beats; strikes (French)

fraternité — brotherhood (French)

golem — a clay creature magically brought to life — and one, in Ashkenazic folklore, that defends the Jewish people from organized Christian violence (Hebrew)

il mio dolce codardo — my sweet coward (Italian)

intaglio — an engraving or incised figure in stone (Italian)

Malpensa — an airport in Milan, Italy

Max Headroom — an AI character introduced in the 1980s. Slick, superficial and self-referential, he's best known for his stuttered catch-phrase, "Catch the wave."

mishpokhe — family (Yiddish)

momser — illegitimate child (Yiddish)

per il mio ex amore — for my former love (Italian)

rodef — pursuer; a fetus posing a risk to its mother's life (Hebrew)

tsimmes — a stew of meat, vegetables and sometimes fruits; confusion (Yiddish)

ACKNOWLEDGMENTS

Some of these poems first appeared — at times in slightly different form — in *American Dream, Blueline, Calapooya, The Carolina Quarterly, Catskill Made, The Common, Contrary, The Cortland Review, Forward, Gastronomica, Harvard Review Online, Hobart, Hospital Drive, Iron Horse Literary Review, J Journal: New Writing on Justice, Journal of Compressed Creative Arts, Judaism, Juked, Lilith, Literary Mama, The Malahat Review, Ninth Letter, North American Review, Opossum, The Pinch, Prairie Schooner, Qu, Rattle, Southern Humanities Review, Spoon River Poetry Review, Subtropics, Tablet, Tikkun, Triquarterly Online,* and *The Tulane Review.*

My gratitude goes to both Kim Verhines and Sandra Carranza of SFA Press for their essential help in bringing this book to print.

ABOUT THE AUTHOR

Author photo by Lana Ortiz

Susan Comninos is a writer and teacher in New York. Her poetry has appeared in *Harvard Review Online, Rattle, The Common, Prairie Schooner* and *North American Review*, among others. She's taught undergraduates at Siena College, The College of St. Rose, and most recently, SUNY Albany, as well as adults in the local community. A graduate of Cornell Univ., holding an MFA in creative writing from the Univ. of Michigan, she works as a freelance writer when she's not in the classroom. Her book reviews, author profiles and literary trend stories have appeared in *The Atlantic Online, The Boston Globe, Chicago Tribune*, and more. She lives near Albany.

CPSIA information can be obtained
at www.ICGtesting.com
Printed in the USA
LVHW040218160422
715918LV00002B/8